THE SALVATION ARMY

Susan Cohen

ENLARGED TO SIXTY-FOUR PAGES

ALL THE WORLD

A REVIEW OF THE WORK OF THE SALVATION ARMY IN EVERY LAND

SOME OF THE PRINCIPAL CONTENTS

THINGS CHINESE. By Commissioner Geo. S. Railton
THE HETERODOXY OF JESUS. By Colonel F. W. Pearce
THE UNITED STATES: A Splendid Year's Record

EVENTS OF THE MONTH
MEMORIES OF ITALIAN SERVICE
IMPRESSIONS AND SKETCHES
THE LATE MISS EMERY
(A Character Study)
THE BRITAIN OF THE SOUTH

IN PERSIA AND ASIATIC TURKEY
GOOD NEWS FROM FINLAND
THE ARMY IN MANCHESTER
KOREA: The Land of the Morning Calm
'THE LIGHT OF INDIA' (Review)
ENTERPRISE IN THE NETHERLANDS

AN ARMY WITH BANNERS. By Nicholas Wills

MAY, 1913   PRICE THREEPENCE

[Registered for the Canadian Magazine Post]

SHIRE PUBLICATIONS

SHIRE PUBLICATIONS
Bloomsbury Publishing Plc

PO Box 883, Oxford, OX1 9PL, UK
1385 Broadway, 5th Floor, New York, NY 10018, USA
Email: shire@bloomsbury.com
www.shirebooks.co.uk

A CIP catalogue record for this book is available from the
British Library.

Shire Library no. 748   ISBN-13: 978 0 74781 245 6

Susan Cohen has asserted her right under the Copyright,
Designs and Patents Act, 1988, to be identified as the
author of this book.

Designed by Ken Vail Graphic Design
Typeset in Perpetua.
Printed and bound in Great Britain.

COVER IMAGE
A Salvation Army band in Halifax, West Yorkshire, c. 1964.

TITLE PAGE IMAGE
All the World has appeared continuously, apart from a break
between 1929 and 1938, at first as a monthly publication,
but later quarterly.

CONTENTS PAGE IMAGE
A 'home from home', where clean, comfortable beds
are supplied, and tasty, wholesome meals are provided
for servicemen.

MIX
Paper from
responsible sources
FSC
www.fsc.org   FSC® C013604

ACKNOWLEDGEMENTS
My thanks to the Salvation Army International Heritage
Centre and to assistant archivist Steven Spencer for help
and advice, and to my friend and mentor Clive Fleay for
sharing his historical knowledge of the Army with me.
Many people gave generously of their help, knowledge
and images, including the Archives and Special Collections
Branch of the Library of the Marine Corps, USA,
Nicky Akehurst, Les Branchett, Chatham SA, Dr Chester
Chu, John Claridge, Jim Crowther, Malcolm Edwards,
Felixstowe SA Archive, Clive Fleay, Jeremy Hague,
Chris Hinton, Glenn Horridge, the International
Concertina Association, Graham Jarvis, Freda Johnson,
Alan Judd, Imelda Kay, Jack Kerr, Will McArthur,
Jon Pater, Arthur Russ and Nathanville Gallery, Howard
Russell, Kevin Sims, Murray Smith, Major Alec Still,
the Salvation Army, Hazel Thorby, Will McArthur, the
Wesleyan Assurance Society of Birmingham, Vivienne
Whitaker and Jim Williams.

IMAGE ACKNOWLEDGEMENTS:
Archives and Special Collections Branch, Library of the
Marine Corps, USA, page 43; Les Branchett, page 34;
Chatham SA, page 41; Dr Chester Chu, page 35 (top);
John Bulmer, front cover image; John Claridge/Akehurst
Creative Management Ltd., pages 51 (top and bottom) and
52; Jim Crowther, page 46; Malcolm Edwards, pages 11
(top), and 38 (bottom right); Mary Evans Picture Library,
page 22; Felixstowe SA, pages 14 (top), 30, 32, 35
(bottom), 39 (top), 41 (top), 43 (top), 50, 56 and 57;
Clive Fleay, pages 3, 6, 7 (right), 10 (bottom), 11
(bottom), 12 (bottom), 15, 19 (bottom), 20, 24, 25 (top
and bottom), 26 and 45 (top); Jeremy Hague, pages 29 and
34; Chris Hinton, page 12 (top); International Concertina
Association, page 33; Graham Jarvis and Captain Howard
Russell, pages 54 and 55 (top and bottom); Freda Johnson,
page 8; Alan Judd, page 24 (top); Imelda Kay, page 47;
Jack Kerr, pages 4, 5, 7 (left), 10, 13 (centre), 28, 36,
38 (right), 40, 49 (top and bottom); Will McArthur/
GlescaPals, page 38 (bottom left); John Pater, page 56
(top); Arthur Russ/Nathanville Genealogy, page 39
(bottom); The Salvation Army, pages 11 (bottom),
13 (top), 21 (bottom), 58 (all), 59 and 60 (both);
Scotia Group Archives (photograph copyright
Alan Walker, Toronto, Ontario), page 48; Hazel Thorby,
page 45; William Trent, page 49 top; Wesleyan Assurance
Society, Birmingham, page 27.

Shire Publications is supporting the Woodland Trust, the UK's leading woodland conservation charity, by funding the dedication of trees.

CONTENTS

EARLY DAYS

T̲HE SALVATION ARMY (SA) was established by William Booth in 1878 and has endured as a remarkable organisation, recognised across the world for its commitment to helping the poor, the friendless and the needy in society. Evangelical Christianity has always been at the heart of the Army and was the driving force behind Booth's decision to create his own church. His mission, as Sir Henry Rider Haggard described in 1910, was 'to try, if not to cure, at least to ameliorate the lot of the fallen or distressed millions ... by ministering to their creature wants and regenerating their spirits upon the plain and simple lines of the New Testament'.

Portrait of the Reverend William Booth by William Joseph Carroll.

William Booth was born in Nottingham on 10 April 1829 and was brought up 'in attendance of the services of the Church of England'. Aged thirteen, he exchanged this for Wesleyan Methodism, which he found 'more interesting', and also started work as an apprentice to a pawnbroker to help support the family. The abject poverty and hopelessness of those he encountered had a profound impact on the young man, and was compounded by the death of his father when William was just fifteen and his family became dependent upon him. By 1849, having been out of work for a year, William had moved to London in the hope of bettering himself, but the only place he could find work was, again, in a pawn shop. As his leaning to the Methodists, and towards radical politics, developed, he was soon spending his evenings preaching to the poor on street corners, just as he had done in Nottingham for the previous three years. On Sundays he would conduct Methodist services wherever he was invited. A chance meeting with one Edward Rabbits provided William with short-term financial support and enabled him to leave pawnbroking and seek a post as a Methodist preacher. Rabbits also introduced William to Catherine Mumford, the young woman who was to become his wife and whose religious and reformist beliefs mirrored his own. The couple became engaged in 1852 but could not afford to get married until 1855.

Years of hardship as an itinerant probationer and then an ordained preacher with the Methodist New Connexion Church followed, but disagreements with the church's leaders, and William's unwillingness to work within the constraints of the circuit system of preaching, impelled the Booths to resign formally in 1862. Unfettered by any authority, William undertook emotional evangelistic campaigns in Cornwall, Cardiff, the Midlands and elsewhere, supported by private sponsorship. The lives of the itinerant couple, who by now had established a strong reputation as revivalists, were dogged by ill health and debt, and in 1865 they moved back to London with their three sons and three daughters, having both accepted invitations to preach. It did not take them long to decide to stay in the city, for they both recognised it offered the best opportunity for reaching the unsaved.

On 2 July 1865 William held his first open-air crusade in Whitechapel at the behest of the publishers of an evangelical weekly, *The Revival*. Having gathered a crowd on the streets, he then preached to them in a tent pitched on a disused Quaker burial ground. In the first two weeks alone, according to a report in *The Revival*, his preaching had attracted between four and five hundred people. As well as disruption caused by troublemakers who cut the ropes, the tent was blown down during a storm in the autumn of 1865, and William realised that alternative accommodation was needed for his newly established East London Christian Revival Union. In the early days, a motley range of buildings was adapted for prayer meetings, including a wool shed, a covered skittle alley known as the Alexandra Hall, and Professor Orson's Dancing Academy in New Road, Whitechapel. Wherever meetings were held, children and adults were converted to Christianity and 'mission stations' appeared all over east London, from Bethnal Green to Limehouse, and from Canning Town to Shoreditch. By 1867 the name had been changed to 'The Christian Mission' and the movement continued to grow, but still relied upon the goodwill of others. The amounts of money donated were carefully noted in William's 1872 report *How to Reach the Masses with the Gospel*, and ranged from the modest to the staggering. One benefactor, Frank Crossley, gave the Army between £60,000 and £70,000 during his lifetime. Advertisements for contributions

Catherine Booth was born at Ashbourne, Derbyshire, on 17 January 1829 and was 'Promoted to Glory' (the SA's exclusive term for the death of a Salvationist) on 4 October 1890.

5

were also included in the Mission's monthly magazine, the *East London Evangelist*, first published in October 1868, and renamed the *Christian Mission Magazine* by January 1870. Costing one penny a copy, it included religious and theological tracts and inspirational stories about the lives of exemplary Christians.

Finding places to hold meetings became an increasing problem, and the Mission was desperately in need of a central meeting place. The first of these, which became the organisation's earliest headquarters, was a run-down beer shop, the Eastern Star, which was acquired for £120. Meanwhile, William was determined to move to a bigger building and began negotiating to buy a building known as 'The People's Market' in Aldgate. The People's Mission Hall, as it was called, eventually opened its doors to the starving poor on William's birthday, 10 April 1870, having cost in excess of £2,750, much of it raised from donations ranging from £250 to as little as a shilling. And what a place the poor encountered, for it had wooden rather than stone floors, and rooms heated by hot-water apparatus, for, as William maintained, 'No one gets a blessing if they have cold feet and nobody ever got saved while they had toothache'. For the next eleven years the building served as the organisation's headquarters, main meeting hall and centre for the distribution of cheap food for the poor, who came from miles around.

William Booth announcing his unwillingness to work within the constraints of the circuit system before resigning from the Methodist New Connexion Church.

It was no accident that William and Catherine's evangelical work – she first preached on her own in 1860, having followed William's Sunday sermons on occasions since 1858 – was localised in east London, for the area was vast and uniformly poor. It had a constantly growing population that was ill served by the existing parish system, and was, as William wrote in 1867, 'a vast continent of vice, crime and misery'. In conducting their preaching the Booths were greatly influenced by the innovative styles used by Charles Finney and James Caughey, two leaders of the American evangelist movement. Their sermons were filled with what *The Revival* had described in July 1865 as 'searching questions, loud warnings, hearty exhortations, Jesus the Saviour from all guilt', while warnings of God's wrath were balanced by promises of a full pardon. And so the crowds grew, and the 1873 Christian Mission Conference, which recorded 901 members at four London Mission stations, was able to report that Whitechapel alone attracted 2,151 people to the twelve meetings held every week. In 1878 seven hundred voluntary workers supported the 127 evangelists who were employed by the Mission. By the following year the organisation had seventy-two stations and had become a national movement spread out across the south coast, the Midlands, the north, the north-east and Wales. Growth brought with it a change in the structure of the organisation, as well as a new name.

Above left: The headquarters of the East London Christian Mission, 1867.

Above right: These sketches depict the rapid progress of the organisation, and the new classes of work it undertook between 1865 and 1882.

THE GENERAL AND STAFF ON CALVARY,
WHERE THE MANIFESTO TO ALL CHRISTENDOM WAS SIGNED.

The Salvation Army
ARTICLES of WAR

TO BE SIGNED BY ALL WHO WISH TO BE ENTERED ON THE ROLL AS SOLDIERS.

Having received with all my heart the Salvation offered to me by the tender mercy of Jehovah, I do hereby now publicly acknowledge God to be my Father and King, Jesus Christ to be my Saviour, and the Holy Ghost to be my Guide, Comforter, and Strength; and that I will, by His help, love, serve, worship, and obey this glorious God through all time and through all eternity.

Believing solemnly that The Salvation Army has been raised up by God, and is sustained and directed by Him, I do here declare my full determination, by God's help, to be a true soldier of The Army till I die.

I am thoroughly convinced of the truth of The Army's teaching.

I believe that repentance towards God, faith in our Lord Jesus Christ, and conversion by the Holy Spirit, are necessary to Salvation, and that all men may be saved.

I believe that we are saved by grace, through faith in our Lord Jesus Christ, and he that believeth hath the witness of it in himself. I have got it. Thank God!

I believe that the Scriptures were given by inspiration of God, and that they teach that not only does everlasting life and the favour of God depend upon continued faith in, and obedience to, Christ, but that it is possible for those who have been truly converted to fall away and be eternally lost.

I believe that it is the privilege of all God's people to be "wholly sanctified," and that "their whole spirit and soul and body may" be preserved blameless unto the coming of our Lord Jesus Christ." That is to say, I believe that after conversion there remain in the heart of the believer inclinations to evil, or roots of bitterness, which, unless overpowered by Divine grace, produce actual sin; but these evil tendencies can be entirely taken away by the Spirit of God; and the whole heart thus cleansed from everything contrary to the will of God, is entirely sanctified, will then produce the fruit of the Spirit only. And I believe that persons thus entirely sanctified may, by the power of God, be kept unblameable and unreprovable before Him.

I believe in the immortality of the soul; in the resurrection of the body; in the general judgment at the end of the world; in the eternal happiness of the righteous; and in the everlasting punishment of the wicked.

Therefore, I do here and now, and for ever renounce the world with all its sinful pleasures, companionships, treasures, and objects, and declare my full determination boldly to show myself a Soldier of Jesus Christ in all places and companies, no matter what I may have to suffer, do, or lose, by so doing.

I do here and now declare that I will abstain from the use of all intoxicating liquors, and also from the habitual use of opium, laudanum, morphia, and all other baneful drugs, except when in illness such drugs shall be ordered for me by a doctor.

I do here and now declare that I will abstain from the use of all low or profane language; from the taking of the name of God in vain; and from all impurity, or from taking part in any unclean conversation, or the reading of any obscene book or paper at any time, in any company, or in any place.

I do here declare that I will not allow myself in any falsehood, deceit, misrepresentation, or dishonesty; neither will I practise any fraudulent conduct, either in my business, my home, or in any other relation in which I may stand to my fellow-men, but that I will deal truthfully, fairly, honourably, and kindly with all those who may employ me or whom I may myself employ.

I do here declare that I will never treat any woman, child, or other person, whose life, comfort, or happiness may be placed within my power, in an oppressive, cruel, or cowardly manner, but that I will protect such from evil and danger so far as I can, and promote, to the utmost of my ability, their present welfare and eternal salvation.

I do here declare that I will spend all the time, strength, money, and influence I can in supporting and carrying on the War, and that I will endeavour to lead my family, friends, neighbours, and all others whom I can influence, to do the same, believing that the sure and only way to remedy all the evils in the world is by bringing men to submit themselves to the government of the Lord Jesus Christ.

I do here declare that I will always obey the lawful orders of my Officers, and that I will carry out to the utmost of my power all the Orders and Regulations of The Army; and further, that I will never allow, if I can prevent it, any injury to its interests, or hindrance to its success.

And I do here and now call upon all present to witness that I enter into this undertaking and sign these Articles of War of my own free will, feeling that the love of Christ, Who died to save me, requires from me this devotion of my life to His service for the Salvation of the whole world, and therefore with now to be enrolled as a Soldier of The Salvation Army.

Signed: *John Andrew Jones*

Corps: *Hanwell*

Date: *January 21st 1904*

BLOOD & FIRE — THE SALVATION ARMY

A NEW ARMY IS BORN

INSPIRATION for the Mission's new name came about, apparently, as William was checking the proofs of the 1878 *Report of the Christian Mission*. Seeing it described as 'a volunteer army', it struck him that his army comprised full-time saviours, quite unlike the soldiers who volunteered for part-time emergency military duty in the regular army. From then on, the Christian Mission became known as 'the Salvation Army', and the *Christian Mission Magazine* was renamed *The Salvationist*. The first person to style himself 'Captain' was Elijah Cadman, an early convert; according to Cyril Barnes, when William was going to hear him, Cadman sent out leaflets announcing that 'the General of the Hallelujah army is coming to Whitby to review the troops – great battles will be fought'. The move towards a hierarchical military-style organisation with its own discipline, newspaper and lexicon evolved as William settled into his new title as 'General' and Catherine became known as 'Army Mother'. Full-time workers were known as 'Officers', and their own paper, *The Officer*, was introduced in January 1893. *Orders and Regulations for the Salvation Army* was published in 1878, with *Orders and Regulations for Field Officers* (ORFO) issued in October 1886, emphasising that 'all positions were open to each alike', regardless of gender. In this, there is little doubt that Catherine's fiercely feminist convictions were instrumental in giving women an equal role within the Army. Members were 'Soldiers' or 'recruits', Mission stations were renamed 'Corps', overseen by a 'Captain', often assisted by a 'Lieutenant', and these were, in turn, divided into districts, under the command of a 'Major'. Several districts were formed into a division, led by a 'Colonel'. The SA also acquired a crest surmounted by a crown, with the Army's motto, 'Blood and fire'. Equally symbolic was the Army flag, and it was Catherine who presented the first corps flag, in Coventry, in September that year.

With so much progress, the new organisation needed its own journal, and the first four-page edition of the weekly *The War Cry*, costing a halfpenny, appeared on 27 December 1879. The SA also required its own training facilities, and in 1880 the first training home in evangelical work began operating from a house in Hackney. It was transferred in 1882 to the old

Opposite: The 'Articles of War'. All new recruits were asked to sign this document before they enrolled as a Soldier; 1907.

A selection of badges, including a medal commemorating William Booth's seventieth birthday in 1899.

Right: A coloured plate used for *The War Cry* being run off at the Army's printing press at Campfield, St Albans, c. 1920s.

London Orphan Asylum in Clapton and for the next forty-eight years the renamed Clapton Congress Hall housed the National Barracks or Training Garrison.

William was initially averse to salvation work with children, but the success of meetings held by Captain John Roberts of Blyth made him rethink his stance. A weekly illustrated children's paper, *The Little Soldier* (later *The Young Soldier*), was introduced in 1881, and William raised

Above: The SA crest and banner designed by William Ebdon in 1878. The motto 'Blood and fire' is a reference to the blood of Jesus and the fire of the Holy Spirit. The 'sun' in the centre represents the light and fire of the Holy Spirit; the crown represents the crown of glory; and the two swords the war of salvation.

Left: Front cover of the American Christmas 1924 edition of *The War Cry*.

Overleaf, top image: An SA family group in uniform.

the issue of the dedication of children at his 1883 New Year address to officers. In the same year a series of his articles on childhood was published in book form as *The Training of Children*, and in 1886 a section on 'Giving Children to the Lord' was included in the *ORFO*, and the Register of the Corps's Children was established.

The rules and regulations of the newly named organisation were set down officially in 1878, leaving no doubt as to the chain of command. William, as General Superintendent, had complete authority for the rest of his life and was empowered to appoint his successor. He also had control of the finances but was obliged to produce an annual balance sheet. Second-in-command was his son Bramwell as 'Chief of the Staff' (or 'Chief of Staff'), assisted by a small band of advisors, including George Railton, who had entered the service of the Mission as its secretary in

Below: Future SA officers at Congress Hall, Clapton, London, where trained officers were commissioned to preach and serve all over the world.

March 1873. Of great importance were, and still are, the *Articles of War*, introduced in 1882, and it became a regulation, in 1890, that 'every soldier must consider, accept and then sign this document' to ensure that he or she was totally committed to the doctrines, principles and practices of the Army. Soldiers were expected to give a weekly offering or 'cartridge' – ammunition to fight the devil.

Left: The 1895 SA Almanac depicts an SA soldier dying, accompanied by an extract from the New Testament: 'I have fought a good fight, I have finished my course. I have kept the Faith.'

Below: Salvationists often wore this distinctive shield-shaped metal badge on their uniform.

Below: *The War Cry* was advertising bonnets for 6s in September 1880. Cheap to produce, long-lasting, protective and plain, the bonnets made in this busy workroom, c. 1920s, were dispatched to all parts of the world.

Missionary float,
Felixstowe, 1925.

The military-style rank system extended to the uniform, which was regularised in early 1880. The first price list, published in *The War Cry* in March 1880, listed a male captain's suit of 'patrol jacket, trousers, collar trimmed with cardinal and the letter S on each side of the neck' at a cost of 21s 6d. The same suit in all-wool diagonal cloth cost 36s 6d. A men's regulation cap was not introduced until 1891. 'Hallelujah lasses', the affectionate name for female soldiers, were recognisable by their large black straw bonnets trimmed with black silk, which were Catherine Booth's idea. Officers and soldiers had to purchase their own outfits and, given that in 1890 a uniform cost, on average, three week's wages, many Salvationists wore theirs whenever possible, including at weddings, funerals and family outings.

This 1892 illustration of William Booth in *St Stephen's Review*, was one of many that appeared in the press, and mocked the concept of the manly, robust Salvationist.

The SA was growing exponentially, with corps established in Scotland and the Channel Islands in 1879. The greatest leap came when the first contingent of SA officers landed in the United States in 1880, with fellow travellers setting up in Ireland and Australia in the same year. Corps were subsequently created in places as distant and widespread as Canada, India, Switzerland and Sweden in 1882, New Zealand, Natal and Zululand in 1883, Jamaica in 1887, Norway in 1888, and Southern Rhodesia (now Zimbabwe) in 1891. This expansion called for a bigger, more central headquarters, and new premises were found at 101 Queen Victoria Street, London, in 1881, which appropriately became International Headquarters (IHQ). In November 1884 another publication, *All the World*, was launched, recording the work of the Army around the globe.

Mobilising the Army also included the use of horse-drawn caravans, first called 'cavalry forts', with such names as 'Faithful', 'Mercy' and 'Rescue'. These travelled the country in the summer months on missions, but, as Cadet William Henderson noted in his diary in July 1891,

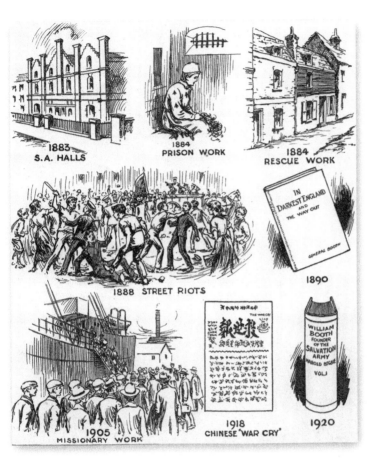

A visual summary
of the 1920s of SA
work from 1883
onwards.

1883
S.A. HALLS

1884
PRISON WORK

1884
RESCUE WORK

1888 STREET RIOTS

1890

1905
MISSIONARY WORK

1918
CHINESE 'WAR CRY'

1920

'Sometimes we get on very well, sometimes we don't, but we do it for the Lord, and he makes it all right'. Caravans were soon replaced by cars, and in August 1904 William, then seventy-five years old, embarked on the first of seven gruelling motor campaigns, spending twenty-nine days travelling from Land's End to Aberdeen, and speaking at 164 meetings in wayside villages and towns.

Against this background of growth, the Army had to face hostility from a number of quarters, including publicans and brothel-keepers who lost business as many of their customers converted. There was organised opposition from the 'Skeleton Armies', named after the skull and crossbones on their flag, who unleashed a reign of terror on marching and preaching Salvationists, using rotting vegetables, dead rats and even burning coal as ammunition. In 1882 alone, 669 Salvationists were brutally attacked in this way, and sixty buildings were torn apart.

DAWNING DAY

PRINTING & PUBLISHING DEPARTMENT, 98, 100 & 102, CLERKENWELL ROAD, E.C.
INTERNATIONAL HEADQUARTERS, 101, QUEEN VICTORIA STREET, E.C.

FOOD AND SHELTER

PREACHING AND RELIEVING POVERTY as a means to salvation soon began to
go hand in hand. The earliest recipients of help were 'fallen' girls,
working as prostitutes, who were offered refuge and reform by Mrs Cottrill,
a Salvationist, in a rented cottage in Hanbury Street in spring 1884. She found
paid washing work for some of them, while others were taught cross stitch
so that they could sew the words 'The Salvation Army' in yellow wool on
the recently introduced uniform red jerseys. For this, Robert Sandall records,
they were paid 3s 6d per dozen, enough to cover rent and buy food, and to
enable a girl to contribute towards her redemption. Soon there were so many
girls and women arriving at the home – eighty-six passed through in the first
year – that The War Cry carried a notice on 25 October 1884 warning officers
not to send girls there without first checking that accommodation was
available. Many of them were pregnant, and in 1886 the officer-in-charge of
the Girl's Rescue Home in Chelsea, London, decided to move her expectant
charges out of the way of the other girls, so the latter were not corrupted.
They went across London to Devonshire Road, Hackney, and this became
the first SA mother and baby home. A year later, in 1887, a maternity
hospital, Ivy House, was opened nearby, with the first student midwife
trained there in 1889, and a nurses' training scheme inaugurated in 1891.
SA officers used Florence Booth's Enquiry Bureau, set up in 1885, 'to follow
up cases of seductions etc.' and endeavoured to 'bring the delinquent to
book'. Some women returned to their families, while others were found
work as domestic servants through the Army network. For the rest, many
were employed in the numerous small industries set up by the Army, which
included a steam laundry and a bookbinding works where copies of All the
World were sewn together. Florence Booth, whom Bramwell had married in
1882, was appointed by William 'to superintend' a special training course
that had been established for rescue officers. According to The Deliverer, there
were ten homes with a joint capacity of 212 spread across Britain in 1890,
and 2,099 girls had passed through their doors.

Opposite:
Front cover of
The Deliverer,
Christmas 1891.
This was the
monthly Army
magazine devoted
to women's social
work, first published
in July 1889.

In the midst of Florence's work among fallen women, the practice of girls being 'trafficked' for immoral purposes came to her and Bramwell's attention. Their revelations led to W. H. Stead's exposé on child prostitution, *The Maiden Tribute of Modern Babylon*, in his *Pall Mall Gazette* in July 1885. The articles played a major role in the raising of the age of consent from thirteen to sixteen, but Bramwell was arrested for alleged involvement. He was subsequently found not guilty and, while the case had been an ordeal, it did serve to raise the profile of the Army and its social work.

Since 1884 SA women cadets of the Cellar, Gutter and Garrett Brigade had been working around Seven Dials in London, helping the poorest children, and two years later a crèche for slum babies was set up in Borough, enabling their mothers to go to work. The plight of hungry children soon resulted in William setting up his 'Farthing Breakfast' scheme for those under sixteen. The scale of the problem was evident from a report in a supplement to *The War Cry* in late 1891 which stated that 'In one large East End school alone it is computed that 700 children attend in a breakfastless condition'. In an effort to provide food for every starving person in London, William opened the first SA Cheap Food Depot in Limehouse, in east London, in 1888. Alongside it, homeless men were offered primitive sleeping arrangements, warm surroundings and an optional prayer meeting in the Army's new night shelter, the 'Threepenny Doss'. More shelters were established in Clerkenwell, Westminster and Whitechapel in 1889 and by 1890 two more food depots were operating, and over three and a half million meals had been served. But even these were not enough to cope with the crisis of a severe winter and in January 1891 *The War Cry* reported that seven emergency relief stations had been set up with the aid of public donations, and were giving out 'between 1,500 and 1,800 half-quartern loaves and an enormous quantity of cheese per day'.

In the hall of the Army shelter for women, 1891.

The first night
in the women's
shelter, May 1891.

Criminals were also well served. For them, William's objective was of 'saving, as far as possible, first offenders from the contamination of prison life'. Seasoned criminals benefited from the Prison Gate Brigade, inspired by the pioneering efforts of two British Salvationists, Major and Mrs James Barker, who made their first prison visit in Melbourne, Australia, in 1883. At home, officers began befriending newly released prisoners, waiting outside the prison

Army officers with
poor children in
the London slums.

gates offering bread and redemption. Devonshire House, Hackney, was operating as the first 'Prison Gate' home by July 1884, and when it was transferred to King's Cross in 1891, under the command of the relocated Barkers, it became known as 'the Bridge', providing accommodation and a workshop. That 135 male criminals had effectively been 'bailed out' by 1894 was a tribute to those involved, from prison governors to chaplains, magistrates, judges, and others who recognised the value of the work. Prison visitation was first initiated in Paisley in Scotland as early as 1889, and the very first SA service for prisoners was held in Plymouth Prison in 1898. Nor were drunkards neglected, with a home for inebriate women opened at Grove House, Upper Clapton, in June 1896, and a retreat for inebriate men at Hadleigh, Essex, in 1901, with others following in later years.

Care for the young continued to expand, with *The Deliverer* reporting in 1901 on the opening of 'The Nest' in Clapton, a home with accommodation for about thirty mothers and thirty children. When the mother and baby home, 'Cotland', was opened in Upper Clapton in 1912, *The Deliverer* delighted in describing the 'airy lightness of each room, the dainty rose budded curtains and cosy white cots'. The Mothers' Hospital in Lower Clapton Road was established the following year and, when war broke out in 1914, it opened its doors permanently to married and unmarried women. During the Second World War the Ministry of Health agreed, under pressure, for the hospital to remain open, on condition that an adequate air-raid shelter was provided. An underground tunnel was completed by October 1940, fitted out, as Ruth Sims, one of the midwives, recalled, with beds for the mothers and long

A meeting in one of the Army's shelters for men.

Selling old clothes in the shelter for women, May 1891.

shelves for babies. Wheelchairs were in short supply, so new mothers were encouraged to be ambulatory two days after giving birth, rather than the usual ten days, so they could walk to the shelter. The exception to the rule were the private patients who paid around 12s 6d for their rooms. One lady, Mrs Levene, who gave birth on 4 December 1942, was very upset to see the other young women, all exhausted from their recent labour, struggling to get to safety while she was pushed in her wheelchair. In all, 6,587 babies were born at the hospital between September 1939 and August 1945.

The cramped air-raid shelter of The Mothers' Hospital during the Second World War. Babies can be seen neatly lined up along the shelf, top left.

THE SUBMERGED TENTH

THE YEAR 1890 was a turning point in Army history, not least because Catherine, William's wife and evangelical partner, was 'Promoted to Glory' on 4 October. If Catherine's death was the end of an era, the publication of William's great manifesto, *In Darkest England and the Way Out*, in late October was the beginning of a new and influential one. The book included graphic accounts of the conditions of the 'submerged tenth', the three million or so desperate and despairing men, women and children who were 'imprisoned for life in a horrible dungeon of misery and despair', and for whom 'the not very tender mercies of the Poor Law system', in particular, had failed. It also detailed a series of permanent schemes to lead England out of darkness, building upon the Army's existing social work. An edition of ten thousand was taken up on the day of publication, and by February 1891 the Publishing Department had issued 175,000 copies.

William's plan divided needy people into self-helping, self-sustaining communities, or 'Colonies', each of which would carry out a process of 'reformation of character' using 'industrial, moral and religious methods'. The first stage was the City Colony, which comprised shelters, or so-called 'dredges', with names like the 'Ark' and the 'Harbour'. Five additional shelters were opened alongside those already existing in London, and another was established in Bristol in 1891, in total supplying 208,019 beds and meals. Temporary employment was provided in factories called 'Elevators', where a progressive system of payment by special tokens enabled men to move upwards from third to first class, with accommodation and payment improving along the way. By the end of 1894 there were seven Elevators in London and the North of England employing one thousand men in industries including carpentry and joinery, French polishing and carpet weaving. But, as *The War Cry* described in March 1891, the most important item in the 'Way Out' of 'Darkest England' was salvage work. The 'Darkest England Salvage Convertor' was opened by William at a Thames wharf in Spa Road, Battersea, in October 1896 and became headquarters of the Salvage Brigade.

Opposite: The frontispiece from *In Darkest England and the Way Out*. The chart was intended to give 'a bird's-eye view of the Scheme described in the book, and the results expected from its realisation'.

Social Wing tokens could be redeemed only at certain places, in order to prevent wages being frittered away on things such as alcohol. The 'FS' may stand for Fieldgate Street.

During one year, small and large dormitories and single cubicles provided 10,912,648 beds in the Army's hostels and shelters.

The second stage was the industrial Farm Colony, which William established on an initial 800 acres of land at Hadleigh, 5 miles from Southend-on-Sea, Essex, in March 1891. The idea of his radical social experiment was to 'give employment (and food and lodgings in return for his labour) to any man who is willing to work, irrespective of nationality or creed'. Within nine months temporary accommodation and facilities had been erected for 'submerged' men and officers, and 215 men were sent from the

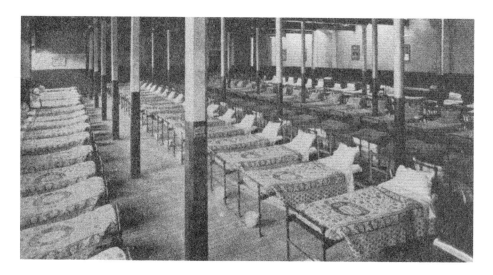

Men returning to Hadleigh colony. Some worked locally, picking strawberries for jam-making at Tiptree Farm. Mr Wilkin, the owner, was so delighted with their work that he helped fund an Army citadel in Hadleigh village.

City Colony. They were taught basic building trades, household work and other handicrafts, and Hadleigh developed into a fully working farm with its own market gardens, orchards, livestock and brickfields. Railway connections and river access enabled produce and supplies to be easily conveyed on SA barges that plied their way up and down the river from the Battersea wharf to the colony. But the scheme was less successful than William had anticipated, for fewer than seven thousand men passed through the colony before the First World War.

In 'Elevators' like this, waste paper and material from private houses, hotels and restaurants were recycled, enabling hundreds of unemployed men to work out their own salvation.

25

This international group of officers, with William Booth and Bramwell Booth, caused quite a stir in London, with their different clothes and unfamiliar accents.

William's Over-the-Sea Colony plan was the third and final stage of the regenerative process, its intention being to settle graduates from the Farm Colony in selected territories abroad. Lack of funds and fierce opposition from the colonial governments prevented the system succeeding, but the emigration scheme for transferring the men abroad did prosper. Assisting emigration was not new to the Army, for it had been helping females to move abroad since 1882, and in 1885 it had published a series of regular advertisements offering free passage for female domestic servants who wanted to work in Queensland, Australia. An SA Emigration Board was established in 1894, the Migration Department was established in 1903, and an Emigration Advice Bureau, which reported weekly in *The Social Gazette*, was set up in 1904. The success of the scheme was evident from the numbers who went overseas – in excess of ninety thousand between 1904 and 1914, of whom only 7,200 were given assisted passage. The demands were so great that by the summer of 1908 new premises in Queen Victoria Street, London, had been secured for the expanding department.

Public interest in the SA was evident by the numbers of people, over 100,000 according to *All the World* in August 1896, who visited the first great exhibition held at the Agricultural Hall, Islington, London, especially since more than half of them were outsiders. There were other innovations within the organisation, including the Naval and Military League (NML), established in 1894 initially as a means of communicating with soldiers and sailors. As the

NML expanded, homes for seamen were set up and became a welcome refuge in ports such as Harwich, Portsmouth and Cardiff, as well as in Calcutta and Malta. The outbreak of the Boer War in 1899 provided an opportunity for the league to expand its boundaries. William appointed Adjutant Mary Murray as assistant secretary of the NML and sent her and a relief party of ten 'welfare' officers to South Africa, to 'minister comfort and practical aid' to both sides in the conflict. Then, as ever, the politics of

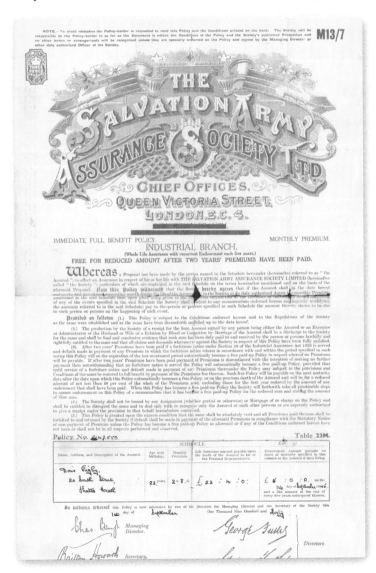

This was the second life assurance policy Mrs Sheffield took out for her daughter Doris, with monthly premiums of 2s 8d. In 1972 Birmingham-based Wesleyan & General, as it was then known, merged with the SA Assurance Society.

27

Self-Denial Week raised nearly £5,000 from Salvationists and ordinary people in 1886, the first year it was introduced, and totalled a record amount of £117,503 in 1918.

'What a beautiful thing is Love! However poor our circumstances, humble our homes, mean and uncultivated our faculties or limited the number of our friends, love can make a heaven in the breast. There is no heaven without it. Love is the essential element of heaven; nor gold, nor fame, nor pleasure, nor friends, nor position can take its place. All are rich who love and are loved. All are poor who possess not love.'

WILLIAM BOOTH

war were irrelevant as the organisation stuck firmly to a neutral position. Apart from making hundreds of hospital visits, Murray and a companion ran a temporary Soldiers' Home from a tent set up as close to the front as women were allowed, and this provided a place where men could go when off duty to 'read, write and get good cheap food'. The League's own journal, *Under the Colours*, was first published in 1897 and continued to report on its activities until 1919.

All of this work required money, but William had already addressed the issue of attracting investments to finance mortgages on property by setting up the Army's own bank in 1890. Acquiring the Methodist and General Assurance Society in 1891 was another big step for the SA, but William viewed life assurance as a social service that was important for the security it provided. The renamed Salvation Army Assurance Society built up its resources slowly and did not take a profit until 1911. By then it had its own journal, *Assurance*, which gave readers free medical advice, on the basis that the longer they lived, the more premiums would be paid. In yet another insurance move, the Salvation Army Fire Insurance Corporation Ltd was registered with the Board of Trade in 1909, and was still operating in 1968. Income was also being generated from Self-Denial Week, first announced in *The War Cry* on 4 September 1886. From 1890 there was the profit from *In Darkest England* and from 'Grace before meat' boxes, introduced in 1893 as a way of collecting regular small sums from members of the newly formed Light Brigade.

By the time the first International Congress was held in 1886, the Army's flag had been unfurled in nineteen countries and colonies, with 1,552 corps, 3,602 officers and 28,200 meetings held every week.

MUSIC AND RECREATION

FROM THE OUTSET music was an essential part of every SA meeting, for it helped convey the gospel message. Hymns were sung and Salvationists played a variety of instruments, including brass and percussion, concertinas and tambourines, renamed timbrels in 1886 at William's request, and it was not long before bands were being formed. The vexed question as to which was the first official SA brass band, that of the Fry family in Salisbury, which consisted of two cornets, one slide trombone and one euphonium, or the first corps band established in Consett, County Durham, in 1879, was eventually settled at an official inquiry in 1906, with Consett being awarded the accolade. Not all members of the Army embraced the brass bands, and, when William informed the captain of the corps in Salisbury that she would have members of the Fry family brass band to help her, she was indignant, crying 'Mr Booth! I don't think I should like it in connection with religious services.' But the value of the band soon became obvious as it effectively drowned out the noise of rabble-rousers. These same troublemakers also targeted the equipment, so

Ripley Songsters, c. 1925. Songsters were Soldiers who were commissioned to sing in Songster brigades, which were originally formed to teach the congregations new songs.

29

Felixstowe Corps band on the beach, 1895.

when the SA began producing its own instruments, first at the IHQ repair shop, and then at its Campfield musical instrument works in St Albans, Hertfordshire, from 1901, they made them with thicker metal to withstand physical abuse. The SA supplied instruments to their bands all over the world until the factory eventually closed in 1972, having lost its competitive edge.

Other early bands included the Household Troops Band, formed in 1887, which toured the United Kingdom for six months before the twenty-five unpaid members travelled to Canada in October 1888 'in the service of God and the Army'. A new band, the International Staff Band, was created in October 1891, and paid its first visit to a prison, Parkhurst, while campaigning on the Isle of Wight in September 1900. There were also drum and fife bands (the fife being a wooden flute), which were cheaper to set up and were well suited to juniors, who might progress to senior brass bands. A number of others started up during the First World War, including one at a convalescent camp at Shoreham, Sussex, and a servicemen's band in Grantham, Lincolnshire, in 1916. The SA Army Motor Ambulance Band, formed from Salvationist personnel, became a welcome feature with the British Red Cross Society, visiting hospitals and SA huts during the First World War, and the music certainly helped to raise the spirits of troops. An unusual group entertained folk in New Basford, Nottingham, during the Second World War, for the Army bandsmen there, about to depart to fight, decided to teach the Salvationist girls how to play so that the band could continue in their absence. The girls went all over the country playing, and on one occasion were away for a whole week and 'got real eggs for our dinner – that was a treat'.

By autumn 1883 William had decided that the only way the Army could have the music and songs he wanted was to produce them itself, and an encounter with Richard (later Lieutenant-Colonel) Slater, a recent convert, provided him with the ideal person to lead this enterprise. For the next thirty years, Slater met the musical needs of the SA, starting with the first Singing Brigade, a combination known as 'the Praying, Singing and Speaking Brigade', made up of Training Home Cadets who toured the country raising funds for training purposes. His job then included finding the voices, teaching the parts and playing the string bass. The Music Editorial Department of the SA was established in October 1883, issuing the SA *Band Journal* and the first *Tune Book* the following year, containing eighty-eight tunes. The monthly *Musical Salvationist* first appeared in July 1886 and included the melodies sung by the Songster Brigades, as the choirs were known. One of the secrets

Advertisements for various SA musical publications in *The Salvationist*, June 1904.

Right: The
Felixstowe Young
People's Singing
Company in 1935.
The group actively
participated in
Sunday meetings
and on other
occasions.

Opposite: Front
cover of *Tutor
for the Triumph
Concertina*, 1938.
This system was
adopted by the
SA in 1912 and
renamed 'Triumph
from Crane'.

of the Army's musical success was its technique of taking well-known music-hall and popular songs and giving them a Christian text. Although the Army does use many traditional hymn tunes, this use of secular popular melodies gives a unique sound to Salvation Army worship.

Seaside promenades and beaches were a popular place for bands to play, and bank holidays an ideal time to get together. In 1908 a visit to Shefford by Leighton Buzzard SA took nearly four hours in an open charabanc drawn by three horses, but they were rewarded with 'every bandsman present, fine weather, good day, good crowds'. Annual Sunday school treats were popular, such as the one held by Sittingbourne Corps in August 1916, which brought together 180 children and about sixty adults who marched behind the band carrying flags and banners on their way to Broom Banks, where they played games and enjoyed a substantial tea. Joy Nixon, a former corps cadet guardian with Leighton Buzzard SA, recalled how Christmas in the 1930s always meant carolling, and how much the corps, and the many long-term patients, looked forward to the band's annual Boxing Day visit to Stoke Mandeville Hospital.

By 1945 there were approximately a thousand senior and a thousand young people's bands in operation, with some fifty thousand bandsmen playing, unpaid, all over the world. In response to changing times, musicals were introduced in the 1960s. The first, *Take Over Bid*, went on stage on 1 October 1966 in front of 1,600 officers of the British Territory gathered at Butlin's holiday camp, Clacton-on-Sea. The response was rapturous, paving the way for many more popular shows. Equally successful was the SA pop group the Joystrings, who for five years between February 1964 and July 1969, under the leadership of Captain Joy Webb, captivated audiences with their spiritual music. The International Staff Songsters were formed in 1980 by

THE SALVATION ARMY
TUTOR
FOR THE
TRIUMPH CONCERTINA

Containing :

Full instructions on the nature and management of the
Instrument, with Exercises and Chords, also a collection
of Hymn Tunes, Solos and Selections, specially
arranged for the Triumph Concertina.

NEW EDITION
Revised and enlarged

Copyright

SALVATIONIST PUBLISHING & SUPPLIES, LTD.,
JUDD STREET, KING'S CROSS,
LONDON, W.C.1

Herbert Hague
(1900–87) was
a committed
Salvationist and a
concertina player
who had some
music published in
the SA *Band Journal*
in the 1950s. He
arranged music
for the SA *English
Concertina Tutor*
published in 1935.
Photograph
c. 1925.

General Arnold Brown, then International Leader of the SA, who challenged the group to inspire people with the 'heart songs' of the SA. Their early recording, *Heart Songs*, includes many SA favourites. With the establishment of the SA Symphonic Wind Ensemble in 1994, the familiar brass bands were joined by Salvationist woodwind instrumentalists and enthusiasts who welcomed the opportunity of performing in an Army environment.

A Salvation Army band playing in Argyll Street, London, 2009.

Poster for *Glory*, one of ten musicals written by the Salvationists John Gowans and John Larsson, composer and lyricist respectively, between 1967 and 1990. *Glory* played to a capacity crowd of nearly one thousand at the Spa Pavilion, Felixstowe, in March 1979.

W. BRAMWELL BOOTH, *General* WILLIAM BOOTH, *Founder* EVANGELINE C. BOOTH, *Commander United States Forces*

JANUARY, 1918

War Service Herald

Vol. VIII. OFFICIAL GAZETTE, WAR SERVICE of the SALVATION ARMY No. 1.

Commander EVANGELINE BOOTH

INTO THE TWENTIETH CENTURY

IN DARKEST ENGLAND continued to impact on social-work schemes in the early twentieth century. In 1905 the Anti-Smoking League (previously the Anti-Tobacco League) was launched, aimed at young lads, followed in 1907 by the Anti-Suicide Bureau, inaugurated at William's behest. According to Rider Haggard, 'in London alone 1,064 cases were dealt with in the year 1909, and of those cases it is estimated that all but about a dozen were turned from their fatal purpose'. William's 1891 intervention in the notoriously dangerous match-making industry bore fruit in the new century. His pioneering of the production of non-poisonous safety matches, using only English materials, in the SA's own match factory in Lamprell Street, led to other manufacturers gradually adopting his practices. In 1901 the SA ceased its involvement and the factory was taken over by the British Match Company. The use of yellow phosphorus was made illegal by a 1908 Act of Parliament.

Other new departures included the Home League, inaugurated by Florence Booth in London in 1907. The SA's women's ministry had a fourfold programme of worship, education, fellowship and service to the community, and was, as Mrs Colonel Catherine Higgins, the first general secretary, described, 'a help-one-another society' and not a mothers' meeting. Concerns for the health and welfare of the elderly poor came to the fore in the early twentieth century, for the state old-age pension, introduced in 1908, was restricted to women over seventy years old, and left many people without support or a roof over their head. The Women's Social Work ministry came up with the germ of a solution by opening so-called 'Eventide Homes', referred to in *The Deliverer* in 1910: 'A small house on the borders of Epping Forest has been secured for the Eventide Home. It will accommodate ten old people. A Slum Officer with a Helper will be in charge. There are many applicants, and it will be difficult to decide between them, for accommodation for ten persons does not go very far!' The first Eventide

Opposite: Eva Booth (1865–1950), William and Catherine's seventh child, was given command in the United States in 1904, changing her name to Evangeline. She became the Army's fourth general on 11 November 1934, the first female to hold the post.

Right: The Home League pledge card with the distinctive emblem of a house on the Bible on the front, had the pledge printed on the back.

Below: This birthday card was sent to Jim Montgomery's family in 1936 by the SA Bridgeton Corps on his second birthday as a reminder that the Army was interested in the baby's welfare, and was waiting to welcome him to the infants meetings.

THE HOME LEAGUE

HOME LEAGUE MOTTO

'She looketh well to the ways of her household'

Prov. 31: 27

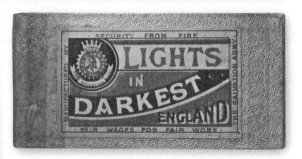

Above: At the same time as the match factory was opened, Booth launched the British Match Consumers' League, urging members to 'worry their grocer, oilman or other shopkeeper, who does not at present stock or sell these matches, at least twice a week, until such time as he does do so'.

A large gathering
of elderly people
enjoying an SA
New Year tea in
January 1926.

Home for aged couples opened in England at Southborough, Kent, in May 1924, followed by the first such home for men in Denmark Hill, London, in July 1926.

When William Booth was 'Promoted to Glory' on 20 August 1912 the whole nation mourned, and as his funeral procession passed through London nine days later hundreds of thousands of working-class people lined the streets to pay their respects. His great organisation, which had now reached fifty-eight countries, passed into the hands of his son Bramwell, and under his command impetus was given to missionary work.

Eva Baglin
(Florence Eveline
Jenner, 1901–84,
second from right)
was the Salvation
Army Singers'
Leader when
Staple Hill SA won
the Home League
Efficiency Banner,
1967.

The Band of Love was started in 1892, as an auxiliary to the Army's junior work, and was a stepping stone to salvation.

As a means of meeting 'the needs of the boy at a time when the problems and possibilities of youth are the greatest', in 1913 the SA created the SA Life Saving Scout Movement for boys aged from eleven to eighteen. This was run on 'certain lines of Scouting carefully adapted to and in harmony with the principles of the Salvation Army' and had a newly combined magazine, *The Warrior and Life-Saving Scout*. Two years later girls were given their own organisation, the Life Saving Guards, and were encouraged to work towards badges such as 'First Aid', 'Athlete' and 'Hostess', which were worn on the arm of their red and grey uniform. On a typical Saturday in Darlington in the 1920s, the girls, led by Commandant Ord, went visiting the workhouse, hospital, sick comrades and old people, taking with them fruit and flowers, which they bought and paid for themselves. Junior groups for children aged from eight to eleven were subsequently set up, the boys' 'Chum Brigade' in 1917 and the girls' 'Sunbeam Brigade' in 1921. For one girl living in Dartford in the 1930s, being a Sunbeam included singing 'Jesus wants me for a sunbeam, to sing and dance each day' at Sunday school, going on train outings, attending concerts at the Citadel, and being given prizes for attendance. In 1906 the first *SA Year Book* was published, as well as a special youth newspaper, *YP*

Life Saving Scouts, like these of the Felixstowe 45 Troop enjoyed healthy recreation, physical development and intensive training in useful crafts; c. 1916.

(renamed *The Warrior* in 1911), which was a careful blend of instruction and religion. Other publications followed: *The Life-Saving Scout and Guard* was introduced in 1921, and renamed *The Scout and Guard* in 1948, the same year that the Life Saving Scouts affiliated with the Boy Scout Association. The *Vanguard,* a thirty-six-page monthly magazine, was introduced in 1956 and promoted the moral, spiritual, physical and educational interests of young people between the ages of fifteen and twenty-one. The Life Saving Guards and Sunbeams lost their exclusive Army link in 1959, when they affiliated with the Girl Guide Association and became Guides and Brownies.

Chatham Life Saving Guards on parade, 1951.

The outbreak of the First World War in 1914 added a new dimension to the Army's activities. At home, officers in their familiar uniform became active on local distress committees, and many cups of tea were served to enlisted men at draughty railway junctions. Nearly three thousand beds were available in hostels and homes in various parts of London and in provincial centres for soldiers passing to and from the front. Women Salvationists could be found travelling day and night on troop trains, blessing and comforting the men, especially those who were wounded, while Home League members visited wives and mothers of SA men. At several military centres they formed sewing and laundry brigades, receiving the soldiers' washing and returning it 'whole and clean'. They also provided thousands of garments, large supplies of chocolate and miscellaneous comforts for the men at the front and for their prisoners of war. The *East Kent Gazette* calculated the cost of all this help at around £3,000 a week in early 1918, and up and down the country War Flag Days were held to raise funds for the maintenance of SA huts, ambulances and hostels, most of them now emblazoned with the familiar red shield symbol, at the front; these catered for 300,000 soldiers every week. The combined efforts of the Sittingbourne and Milton Regis corps raised over £59 in June 1918 for this cause.

There were successive gifts of motor ambulances for service with the Red Cross, with the initial fleet of five dedicated at the London Guildhall on 1 December 1914, and a total of thirty ambulances, most driven by Salvationists, served at home and in

'Chums' were taught 'useful lessons for body, mind and soul'; c. 1920s.

the war zones abroad. One driver was Fred Ireson, who, according to his great grandson, marooned his ambulance on a beach in France and was nearly swamped by the rising tide. General Bramwell Booth presented him, and other members of the Motor Ambulance Band, with an inscribed euphonium in recognition of their war service. By July 1916 there were fifty thousand serving Salvationists, and 350 men had been killed in action. Among them was twenty-three-year-old James Henry Fynn, of the 4th Battalion South Wales Borderers. Sent out to the Middle East in November 1915, he was involved in the campaign in Mesopotamia (now Iraq). While under constant enemy fire, he repeatedly left the advanced trench to rescue several wounded men. Fynn was killed on 30 March 1917, and his courageous sacrifice was recognised in the summer of 1917, when he was posthumously awarded the Victoria Cross, the nation's highest award for gallantry. Two other Salvationists, William Clamp and Thomas Holmes, were similarly decorated for wartime acts. However, it was not until 1920, three years after the Order of the Founder was instituted

by General Bramwell Booth, that the first such award was made – to Private Herbert J. Bourn, for outstanding Christian witness and service during military service in the First World War. In the midst of the conflict William Booth's dying wish, that the SA become established in China, came to fruition, with the first services held in Shantung in 1916, and when famine struck that country in the 1920s the SA saved many lives, feeding 100,000 people every day.

'Sunbeams' were the equivalent of the Brownies and had a yellow and grey uniform.

Photographed at the front line in France, c. 1917, Salvationists Helen Purviance and Margaret Sheldon (on the right) were appointed to the First Division at Montiers-sur-Saulx by October 1917 and introduced doughnut making, improvising with an empty bottle as a rolling pin. They were often under bombardment by German guns. The 'doughnut girls' also sewed buttons, mended uniforms, talked and listened, sang, preached and prayed. (Adolph Bradlee Miller Collection, box 4, folder 1.)

THE 1920s ONWARDS

IN THE AFTERMATH of the First World War a new organisation, the international Red Shield Club, was created for Salvationist servicemen, with headquarters in London, but the Naval and Military Homes in Britain retained their original title until after 1947, when they became Red Shield Services League Hostels.

The Army's interest in the spiritual and social welfare of everyday folk had been taking London Salvationists to the hop fields of Kent in the late summer months from as early as 1886, a practice that resumed after the end of the First World War. *The War Cry* recorded how, from the 1920s onwards, officers were on station platforms at 3.30 a.m. on the day of departure, helping the pickers and their families on to the trains. They set up their headquarters at an SA-owned cottage in Yalding, taking care of the children in a makeshift crèche from seven in the morning until early evening, feeding, entertaining and cleaning up to forty babies and toddlers. Officers trundled rudimentary carts around the fields serving refreshments, while a daily clinic in the first-aid hut provided basic medical care. By the late 1960s manpower was replaced by mechanisation in the hop fields, bringing this valuable branch of SA work to an end.

The work of the Emigration Department, curtailed during the war years, received a huge boost following the introduction of the 1922 Empire Settlement Act, which provided government-assisted passage for migrants, and land settlement schemes. By 1938 the scheme had helped nearly 250,000 people settle abroad. Among them were many youths aged fourteen to nineteen, destined initially for Canada, and from 1927 for Australia, who had participated in the SA's innovative six-week Boys' Training Scheme run at Hadleigh Farm. The scheme continued until the outbreak of the Second World War.

1929 was an important date in SA history, for in February that year Bramwell Booth was deposed as General by a High Council comprising the sixty-three most senior Army officers, and General Higgins was elected to replace him. Weeks later, on 16 June, Bramwell was 'Promoted

A party of young farmers off to New Zealand, c. 1920s, as part of the Army's Boys' Migration Scheme, an adjunct to William Booth's migration scheme, launched in 1903.

to Glory', aged seventy three, shortly before William Booth College, Denmark Hill, London, was opened by HRH Prince George, Duke of Kent, on 8 July. The building, designed by Gordon and Viner, with Sir Giles Gilbert Scott as consultant, served as a memorial to the founder, and henceforth became the heart of the organisation.

During the 1920s and 1930s SA work was begun in numerous African countries, as well as in Bolivia, Germany, Latvia, Hungary, Surinam, Brazil, Estonia and Curacao, among others. In 1930 General Evangeline Booth

A Salvation Army soup kitchen in Darwen, Lancashire, c. 1933–6.

A *Punch* Christmas
fund-raising appeal,
1933.

The Spirit of Christmas

finds a natural home
in The Salvation Army

146,000 of those in Great Britain who
think God and man may have forgotten them
will this Christmas have a happy surprise.

No less than 146,000 are to make merry at
The Salvation Army. Plans are complete.
In 1,000 of its Halls, Shelters, Homes, etc.,
tables will be spread and entertainment
arranged for what will be, in all, one of
the largest Christmas treats ever given.

The Salvation Army

is launching out in this big additional expenditure
because it has faith in the Spirit of Christmas in
you. 2/- provides a treat for one. £50 provides
for 500. Please send gifts to-day marked
"Christmas Cheer," to General E. J. Higgins,
101, Queen Victoria Street, London, E.C.4.

inaugurated the Order of the Silver Star, whose purpose was to recognise
and honour each mother (by natural birth or legal adoption) whose son or
daughter was commissioned as an officer in the Salvation Army. The award
was extended worldwide in 1936.

When Britain became a temporary safe haven for child refugees from
the Spanish Civil War in 1937, the SA was the first organisation to offer them
asylum, undertaking to take four hundred children. Food and clothing cost
about £1,000 per week but Salvationists and sympathisers, including George
Bernard Shaw, contributed generously to cover these expenses. Some of the
Basque evacuees were sent to Hadleigh Farm, where a young Salvationist,
Brindley Boon, was asked to organise games and entertainment each
Saturday. The SA was very sensitive to the children's religious beliefs and
made arrangements with the local Catholic priest, who held Sunday Mass
for the children in the SA hall.

In the Second World War Salvationists mobilised again, with activities at
home providing support both for the general population and for the troops.
SA mobile canteens were an improvement on the earlier travelling food
kitchens; they attended more than five hundred V1 and 120 V2 bomb
incidents in the Greater London area alone, supplying on-the-spot
refreshments to over half a million people. They travelled to isolated
anti-aircraft emplacements and barrage balloon defences, provided canteens
on the overnight trains between England and Scotland, and took basic
refreshments to the thousands who slept on London Underground station
platforms. A Home League in Orkney was able to send £10 to the Wool
Fund, and Salvationists and friends in Canada knitted three thousand

Advertisements like these appeared regularly in the British press.

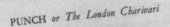

garments for evacuee children in the British Isles. Hadleigh Farm again provided a safe haven for refugees, this time to seventy Jews fleeing persecution in Nazi Europe, but when some parts of the Farm Colony were requisitioned by the military they had to return to London. International Headquarters was destroyed by enemy bombing in May 1941, but the Canadian Red Shield stepped in and offered the use of its hostel in Southampton Row, London. By August 1941 wartime restrictions had reduced the size of *The War Cry* to just four pages, and, in recognition of the part played by non-Salvationists in furthering the work of the SA, a new award, the Order of Distinguished Auxiliary Service, was instituted in February that year. With nurses playing such an important role in wartime, the inauguration of the SA Nurses' Fellowship in 1943 was inspirational, for it enabled Salvationist nurses to keep in touch with Army activities and gave them a place where they could rest and refresh.

Enemy-occupied lands were a very different matter, and the work of the Army was suppressed in Estonia, Italy, Japan, Korea and Latvia. Many

Mobile tea canteen presented to the SA by members of the Bank of Scotia's general office, 25 June 1941.

A 1943 poster appealing for funds to help the SA offer welfare services overseas.

WHERE THERE'S NEED —

'WEAPONS FIRST—But Welfare must follow'

THE Red Shield of The Salvation Army, familiar to the millions of Servicemen and women who find a second "home", in Salvation Army Clubs, Leave Hostels, Guest Houses and Canteens, in Great Britain, is well known, too, in SICILY, NORTH AFRICA and THE MIDDLE EAST, in New Guinea, Ceylon and India. Wherever they find The Salvation Army sign, men and women of the Forces know that it represents friendly service, Christian standards, and a link with home.

NEW FRONTS MEAN EVEN GREATER DEMANDS

Workers and equipment must be ready to follow the Services. Money is urgently needed for this work—now!

PLEASE SEND A GIFT TO-DAY TO:—

GENERAL CARPENTER
101, QUEEN VICTORIA STREET, LONDON, E.C.4

THERE'S THE SALVATION ARMY!

THE ARMY THAT SERVES ON EVERY FRONT

male Salvationists were captured and sent to Germany for forced labour. Serving officers in the Army in France were made prisoners of war, and one officer, Major Georges Flandre, was shot, betrayed by a man whom he had befriended. Damage to Army buildings in France was extensive, and in 1941 alone seventeen Red Shield clubs, twenty-six other buildings with canteens and sixteen canteen ambulances were lost. The Army did what it could to oppose German anti-semitism and, when the campaign against the Jews intensified in Norway in the autumn of 1942, the Army joined with the churches, unsuccessfully, in declaring such racial discrimination to be a contradiction of both the Christian gospel and the historic practice of the Norwegian people.

Even before peace was declared in Europe in May 1945, the SA post-war relief teams had started to move into parts of Germany, and Swedish relief teams were getting emergency supplies into northern Norway.

Second World War Salvation Army badge.

THE POST-WAR ERA

ITH THE United Kingdom returning to normal after the Second World War, the SA held the first International Youth Leaders' Conference in August 1948, followed two years later by the first International Youth Congress, attended by 1,200 delegates. A property in south London was adopted in 1950 to house an international college for officers, and in the same year the SA Students' Fellowship, which had spread since it was started in Norway in 1942, was officially constituted and soon had branches in five continents. The first international Salvation Army scout camp was held at Lunteren in the Netherlands in August 1952. By the time the Home League celebrated its fiftieth anniversary in 1957, it had 277,000 members worldwide. The rebuilt International Headquarters was declared open by Queen Elizabeth the Queen Mother on 13 November 1963, and in 1965 her daughter, Queen Elizabeth II, was in attendance at the commencement of the International Centenary on 24 June. Two thousand

The Torchbearer Youth Movement catered for both Salvationist and non-Christian young people aged between fifteen and thirty. A group was commenced in Felixstowe in 1945 and the members enjoyed table and board games, guest speakers, social evenings, drama, and, in the summer, outdoor pursuits such as cycling and organised games. Here they are decorating the upstairs primary room of the SA premises, c. 1945.

delegates gathered in Westminster Abbey on 2 July for the Founder's Day Service, and in an historic ceremony the Abbey accepted custody of a memorial to William Booth. Her Majesty the Queen was in attendance again in 1968 when she officially opened Booth House, Whitechapel, a new venture providing shelter for homeless single men and vagrant alcoholics, with an eleven-bed referral assessment centre. Two British Salvationist policemen, Paul Hunter and Bob Cameron, were the driving force behind the establishment in 1974 of the Blue Shield Fellowship, and within four years this group had become international. The SA Nurses' Fellowship also extended its remit and in 1975 was renamed the SA Medical Fellowship, open to all those engaged in the healing ministry, regardless of creed. From 1 April 1978 the individual social services for men and women were combined under one management, and the Darkest England Scheme became known as the Social Trust Deed. The SA Migration Department, established in 1903, became Reliance World Travel Ltd in 1981, and finally closed its doors on 31 May 2001. The 1983 *SA Year Book* listed almost one hundred British prison establishments that were regularly visited by the SA chaplaincy service. By the time the Mothers' Hospital closed in 1986, 123,909 live births had been recorded and 3,119 nurses, including 278 full-time SA officers, had been trained there. William Booth's scheme to

Salvationists at Victoria Home, 177 Whitechapel Road, in 1982. The men's hostel opened in 1919 and closed in 1984.

A resident of Hopetown Women's Hostel, east London, in 1982. In 2012 the hostel provided accommodation for ninety-nine women in need of support, including those with mental health and substance abuse issues.

51

A homeless man
outside Booth
House in 1983.
Booth House
provides quality
supported
accommodation,
with staff cover
twenty-four hours
a day, for 150 single
homeless men aged
over eighteen who
have a history of
rough sleeping.

retrain the unemployed and marginalised in society continued and, as an adjunct to Hadleigh Farm, the Army opened Hadleigh Training Centre in 1990, providing training in contemporary skills for people with special educational needs, enabling them to obtain work. *The Young Soldier* was reinvented in 1996 as a weekly newspaper of eight to twelve pages called *Kids Alive!*

Just as in October 1913, when Army officers and soldiers responded to Britain's worst ever mining accident, at Senghenydd, South Wales, joining the search parties, while others supported and comforted mothers and wives, so they came out in force when Pan American Flight 103 was brought down by a terrorist bomb over Lockerbie, Scotland, in December 1998. Mobile kitchens were set up as part of the emergency operations, with food donated by the local shop, and professional SA counsellors were on hand to provide emotional and spiritual support.

CONTINUING WILLIAM BOOTH'S VISION

Life with dignity, equality for all people and a world without poverty and injustice. (The Salvation Army Vision, 2012)

THE SALVATION ARMY'S worldwide mission, which is both proactive and reactive, reaches out to any national or international community that looks to it for support. In the United Kingdom, in 2012, the SA was one of the largest providers of social care after the government, caring for and about individuals from cradle to grave. Nationally, facilities for children include day nurseries, pre-schools, playgroups and crèches for children aged between nought and five, all of which are available to everyone. Breakfast clubs (a modern version of William's 1891 'Farthing Breakfasts'), an after-school homework club and holiday clubs, as well as the child contact centres and the residential family and youth centres, provide safe havens and specific support. Locally, individual churches run family-focused community activities such as parent and toddler groups, arts and crafts and musical activities.

In the United Kingdom the Army is foremost in caring for homeless people, and, to minimise the enduring stigma of being in such a place, its hostels have been renamed 'Lifehouses'. These continue to offer more than a bed and they work hard at helping people to lead fulfilling and independent lives. Recognising that drug addiction and substance abuse are major contributory factors to homelessness, the organisation has numerous centres around Britain where treatment and practical support are given. For those who find themselves unemployed, there are wide-ranging specialist services aimed at helping people find work. When Florence Booth established her Enquiry Bureau in 1885, she could not have foreseen that it would still be in operation more than a century later as the SA Family Tracing Service, which reunites more families than any other agency in the United Kingdom.

Ever since the first Eventide Home was opened in 1910, the SA has cared for the elderly, a tradition that continues in the twenty-first century. Church and community centres offer a wide range of day-care activities, facilities and services, and there are residential homes and support services to enable independent living.

None of this work could continue without financial support, to which the SA charity shops, Christmas appeals and recycling activities contribute. In 1991 International Headquarters was restructured as a separate entity from the United Kingdom Territory, and in the same year the SA Trading Company Ltd was set up. Besides distributing over 400,000 door-to-door collection bags each week, this venture has over five thousand textile recycling banks and more than 120 charity shops nationwide.

William's 'poor man's bank' was renamed 'Reliance Bank' and continues to practice ethical banking, with investments made only within strict moral boundaries, with allowable profits used to advance the evangelical and charitable work of the SA. The SA General Insurance Company now exists as a wholly owned subsidiary of the SA, with the profits going to the organisation.

MPs and peers were invited to the SA's Soup Kitchen Challenge in November 2009. Soup and a roll were provided in return for a donation to the work of the Army.

The SA emergency response team and vehicle at King's Cross station on 7 July 2005 in response to the London bombings.

Booth House in Whitechapel underwent a complete refurbishment and was reopened by the Queen in 2002; it can now accommodate 150 homeless single men over the age of eighteen.

The SA emergency services continue to operate worldwide and their trained officers are often among the first on the scene when disaster strikes. Following the terrorist attacks on 11 September 2001 in New York, the SA was the first relief agency to reach Ground Zero, and its relief workers remained at the World Trade Center site until operations officially concluded

The Army was on hand serving refreshments at St Pancras station in December 2010 when Eurostar services were cancelled because of snow, and hundreds of people were left stranded.

A 'drumhead' ceremony, London, 2011. The band's bass drum acts as the 'mercy seat' or 'penitent form'. People kneel at the drum and 'claim salvation'.

in May 2002. In the aftermath of three hurricanes in the United States in 2005 and 2008, the SA helped evacuate people and provided them with temporary accommodation and financial aid. The SA mobilised resources and personnel to assist with the international relief effort following the catastrophic earthquake in Haiti in January 2010, as it had after the tsunami of Boxing Day 2004.

Since the 1980s, the SA has run a global holistic HIV/AIDS programme, 'A Cry in the Darkness', which cares for people's physical, practical, spiritual

Folk enjoying a nice cup of tea after their Christmas lunch in 2008. The event has been a regular feature of Felixstowe SA's OUTREACH programme for many years. The only qualification for attending is that a person will be lonely at Christmas. In 2012, over seventy people enjoyed a meal.

and emotional needs. Victims of human trafficking, a present-day form of slavery, both at home and abroad, can depend upon the Army for support, safe accommodation, legal advice, counselling and health care, and the careful restoration of freedom and dignity.

Protecting the environment is addressed through the 'Earth' scheme, while 'Embrace' runs an extensive range of community support programmes for orphans, giving hope and a future to the world's most vulnerable children. The more than one billion people around the world, mostly poor farmers, who go hungry are not ignored, and donations to 'Farm' support them by giving them 'the tools, training and techniques they need to make the best use of their land and grow enough food to support their families'. The Army has water projects in over eighteen regions around the world, and its International Emergency Services team runs drought relief projects in countries including Kenya and Australia.

In 2012 the Army was running 183 health programmes in thirty-nine countries, focusing on healthcare and the prevention of disease. These include twenty-three general hospitals and more than 150 clinics and health posts, ranging from the Pitanka Health Post, serving three thousand people in six villages across the mountainous Highlands region of Papua New Guinea, to fifteen hospitals in India and Indonesia. The Army offers education programmes that equip health workers with appropriate skills and experience as well as developing commitment to holistic Christian health ministry.

The Felixstowe corps, with dancers and musicians, taking part in the 2007 Carnival themed 'mardis gras' (party). The banner proclaiming 'No God? No Peace? - Know God! Know Peace!' remained on display in the town for several days.

Above: Front cover of *All the World* celebrating the centenary of William Booth's 'promotion to glory', July to September 2012 issue.

Above: Linda Bond, the General of the SA, in Ghana at a painting presentation by Kofi Ronald, an SA soldier and resident of the Army's Begoro Rehabilitation Centre, 9 February 2012. Kofi has cerebral palsy and uses his mouth to paint.

Left: Linda Bond with children of training college staff, India South Eastern Territory, 1 August 2012.

William Booth College remains at the heart of SA education and learning programmes, and, as a way of inspiring spiritual renewal and rejuvenating interest in the SA, 'Roots' conferences are held across the United Kingdom Territory. Today, most Army corps have their own band; Captain John Mott, an Army bandsman who carried the Olympic torch through Hatfield Peverel, Essex, on 6 July 2012, recalled how the experience was 'very humbling'. John Willson, another Olympic torchbearer, nominated for his contribution to bringing the sport of archery to thousands of young people across Britain, was loudly cheered as he passed in front of the regional offices of the Army, the organisation for which he first started to teach archery to young people through its scouting groups in Hadleigh, Essex.

The spirit of the early Prison Gate brigade still exists, and the Army retains a strong commitment to working with prisoners. Its chaplains are in post in many prisons in the United Kingdom, giving anything from a few hours a week to full-time work.

Well over 120 years have passed since William Booth embarked upon his great mission to defeat poverty and injustice, and to empower people to achieve and maintain a better life. All the services the Salvation Army provides are, in the words of Commissioner Robert Street, 'geared to the

The Salvation Army Mission Statement.

Vision Plan

ONE ARMY — moving forward together — convinced of our calling, — into the world of the hurting, broken, lonely, dispossessed and lost, reaching them in love by all means — with the transforming message of Jesus, bringing freedom, hope and life. — We see a God-raised, Spirit-filled Army for the 21st century

ONE MISSION

ONE MESSAGE

WE WILL ...
● deepen our spiritual life
● unite in prayer
● identify and develop leaders
● increase self-support and self-denial

WE WILL ...
● emphasise our integrated ministry
● reach and involve youth and children
● stand for and serve the marginalised
● encourage innovation in mission

WE WILL ...
● communicate Christ unashamedly
● reaffirm our belief in transformation
● evangelise and disciple effectively
● provide quality teaching resources

A Salvation Army officer on Oxford Street, London.

challenge of the local situation', and it recognises the need to move with the times. In the United Kingdom Territory, Catherine Booth's distinctive bonnet has gone and been replaced with a bowler-style hat, and the uniform now includes hooded tops, polo shirts and combat trousers. But no matter what clothes the individual Salvationist wears, today's Army marches on, as the *2012 Year Book* observed, because 'it has never depended on one man or one woman – however visionary or gifted. It depends on God'.

A Salvation Army officer with one of the many homeless and vulnerable people whom the organisation helps in the UK and across the world.

FURTHER READING

Barnes, Cyril. *God's Army*. Lion Publishing, Berkhamsted, 1978.

Booth, William. *In Darkest England and the Way Out*. Book Jungle, 2008. (Also available to download free of charge on Kindle from Amazon www.amazon.co.uk/Darkest-England-Way-Out-ebook).

Brooks, Stephen. *God's Army. The Story of the Salvation Army*. Channel 4 Books, 1998.

Chesham, Sallie. *Born to Battle. The Salvation Army in America*. Rand McNally, Chicago, 1965.

Cook, Graham, and Parker, Gordon. *Hadleigh Salvation Army Farm: A Vision Reborn*. Salvation Army, 2008.

Cox, Gordon. *The Musical Salvationist: The World of Richard Slater (1854–1939)*. Boydell Press, Woodbridge, 2011.

Fairbank, Jenty. *Booth's Boots. Social Service Beginnings in the Salvation Army*. Salvation Army, 1983.

Horridge, Glen. *The Salvation Army Origins and Early Days 1865–1900*. Abernant, London, 2013.

McKinley, Dr E. H. *The Salvation Army, Including Marching to Glory: The History of The Salvation Army in the United States, 1880–1980*. Harper & Row, 1980.

Larsson, John, and Georges, Berni. *1929. A Crisis that Shaped the Salvation Army*. Salvation Books, London, 2009.

Le Feuvre, Catherine, and Ruthven, Leanne. *Portraits: A Month in the Life of the Salvation Army*. Shield Books, 2012.

Walker, Pamela J. *Pulling the Devil's Kingdom Down. The Salvation Army in Victorian Britain*. University of California Press Ltd, 2001.

Watson, Bernard. *A Unique Society, a History of the Salvation Army Assurance Society Limited*. Salvationist Publishing, London, 1968.

Williams, Dr Harry. *An Army Needs an Ambulance Corps. A History of the Salvation Army's Medical Services*. Salvation Army, 2004.

Yee, Lieutenant-Colonel Check-Hung, O. F. *Good Morning China – The Chronicle of the Salvation Army in China 1916-2000*. Crest, USA, 2005.

WEBSITES

The official United Kingdom Salvation Army website has a wealth of information about all aspects of the movement at www.salvationarmy.org.uk. The international website can be found at www.salvationarmy.org. Individual countries have their own websites, which can be located via a Google search. Books on aspects of the SA can be found at the SA Bookshop website: www.sps-shop.com

The SA International Heritage Centre is the major repository of material relating to the history of the movement, and the collections comprise a library, archive and museum. An appointment is needed to use the archives and library. SA International Heritage Centre, William Booth College, Champion Park, London SE5 8BQ; telephone 020 7326 7800 or email heritage@salvationarmy.org.uk.
Website: www.salvationarmy.org.uk/uki/heritage

The 'Look 4 Them' website (www.look4them.org.uk) is the joint initiative of six organisations in the United Kingdom, including the SA, set up to make it easier to find help and advice in tracing people.

For the SA Historical and Philatelic Association (SAHPA) visit http://sahpa.blogspot.co.uk or contact Dr Glenn Horridge, Chairman, SAHPA, glenn.horridge@virgin.net

Felixstowe SA Corps Archive (www.felixsa.org.uk) has a vast collection of images dating back to 1887 and depicting the social history of the corps from the early founding years to the present day.

The history and images of Chatham SA Corps from 1890 can be found at www.chathamsa.org.uk/history/story

Information on the SA Mothers' Hospital can be found on http://health.hackneysociety.org

Nathanville Genealogy website has a large collection of images from Staple Hill SA Corps: www.nathanville.org.uk/gallery/index.php

For the SA images of John Claridge visit www.johnclaridgephotographer.com and *Spitalfields Life* at http://spitalfieldslife.com/2012/10/01/at-the-salvation-army-in-the-eighties; also spitalfieldslife.com/2012/05/07/john-claridge-at-the-salvation-army/

SAWiki.net is an unofficial online encyclopedia covering all aspects of the Salvation Army: www.sawiki.net

PLACES TO VISIT

Heilsarmee Museum Basel is a private museum about the Salvation Army in
Basel, Switzerland. Visits are by appointment with C. Fässler, Hechtweg 5,
CH-4052 Basel, Switzerland. Telephone/fax: 041 61 312 03 72.
www.heilsarmeemuseum-basel.ch/E/index.php

Salvation Army Museum, SA International Heritage Centre,
William Booth College, Champion Park, London SE5 8BQ.
Telephone: 020 7326 7800. Email: heritage@salvationarmy.org.uk.
Website: www.salvationarmy.org.uk/uki/heritage. The SA has
produced a London walk following in the footsteps of William
Booth, which can be found at www.salvationarmy.org.uk/uki/
Whitechapel_Walkabout

The William Booth Memorial Museum, William Booth Memorial Complex,
Notintone Place, Sneinton, Nottingham NG2 4QG.
To arrange a visit, please telephone 0115 950 3927.

An internet search for 'Salvation Army heritage centres' will provide a
list of worldwide heritage centres, museums and archives in Australia,
Brazil, Canada, Bermuda, New Zealand, Norway, Iceland, the Faroes,
Switzerland and the United States.

INDEX